to, day and night

-nandini tiwari

as long as we live
there is more
for those who
embrace acceptance
and strive to do more

here's to you
always choosing you
even if i don't

hello

for all those who let me dream, this isn't just about me
but about us.

readers are left to verify poetry, so what may be lust for
me (while I burn) might be pleasure for you (to live).

this year again I put in hours to squeeze every drop to
live and help you a bit.
this book may confuse you with words such as forever;
seek answers that resonate with you. all i can promise is
that your light will always be by your side.

our thoughts are contained in *"to, day and night,"* even in
those which might sometimes be embarrassed to admit
when sacrificing pleasure for responsibilities.
"to, day and night" would be nothing without your desire
to believe in something better. It is not for you to change
but for you to bloom.

*for the ones I could match love me or hate me, here are
some poems I promise will be special.*

contents

begin

nobody can figure out
how value is a divine longing
that voids
the beginning and the end

to. day and night

storms create hope in the silence of growth

to. day and night

lust is the pleasure
that talks about
one belonging to another
in tears ripping both hearts apart
asking for the same in return
for all to pass and none to win

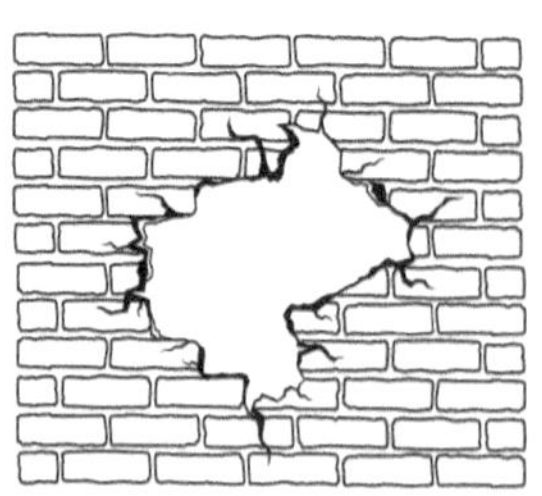

to. day and night

long before you and i
i would teach myself
to not be
needy
easy or
weak

to, day and night

even if you managed
to make that 2am speech
it will sound like a responsibility
without drowning
in your heart and in their eyes

(hold on to it)

to. day and night

despite knowing new people
by the decade
worship the thunder
to bloom and provide you light
to change in a way
that is acceptable

life is all about you and your strength

to. day and night

you held my heart
with a naked mind
snagged in the trauma
of a young child

to. day and night

welcome wisdom to unlock
the real treasure distracted
by your lover

to. day and night

trying is progress
words don't rush
for you are in control

in control of performance
to be *unique*

to. day and night

NANDINI TIWARI

even if i managed to
trap your presence
like a suitcase full of clothes
i'd be left feeling empty
in between the whites
until we unite

need you hear
by my side

to, day and night

in the presence of passion
evolving is a beautiful story
it's what you do to me unmasked
while i escape the past

NANDINI TIWARI

i lie in bed each night
decorating my responsibilities
with commitments
wrapped in the words of my parents
so that the following day
is all about comfort

to. day and night

NANDINI TIWARI

from one end to the other
the permission left me empty
i couldn't process
my progress ahead
and all i felt was suffocation

to, day and night

NANDINI TIWARI

my heart wants to crawl
into their arms
to realize how scared i should not be
once i own it
i will let go of hatred
and enter a world of joy

am i being selfish?

with my eyes
searching the world with colours
i realise that our souls dance the same

to. day and night

would you love me enough
to escape the visions of disappointment
and turn them into a night
with the energy of the invisibles
for my heart deserves a reset

?

to, day and night

take me by my hand
in the silence of touch
in your *magic of lust*

to. day and night

music cannot come through
his charm
of absolute devotion
towards the power of flight

love makes me proud
to live in a world
where the seven colours
of the rainbow
are woven together by your voice

to, day and night

NANDINI TIWARI

i am still learning
to surrender with the stars
the imaginary love
that i have slept with all my life
is trapped with the secret of my heart

wild and beautiful
drenched in the memory
i will never forget being a part of you
as the scars yet scream you

error

we've worked so hard
to look ridiculous and unbecoming
to run in the constant cycle of lust

to. day and night

it would be possible
to know so much more
if love were like thoughts

in love
she fulfilled the promises
that she couldn't afford

silly was a man who never sought happiness

to, day and night

i wish i knew extra warmth
could even frighten
love and the season change

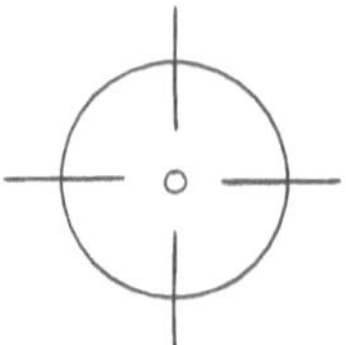

..but, the error now lies within us
as we sit back staying the same
with the smirk of a dying rose
beneath the rays of sunlight
hiding behind the opportunities
like they are not meant for us

to. day and night

you fear the moon
because of the silence you share with it
which you think is strong enough to carry
your most painful cries and screams

but darling
the loss of breath and lack of words
are your real enemies

to. day and night

NANDINI TIWARI

but deep within my mind
the reflections of you yet stay
spiralling out like tentacles
in my dreams
you make an appearance
trying to seek refuge
in thousands of those cramped spaces

to. day and night

dreams fall in love
with the kind of conversations
that the writers complete
and the people believe

to. day and night

if i had known
that every day i'd like to
laugh with you
i would stop dreaming about tomorrow
and forever just live
in present instead

to. day and night

loneliness is blamed for touch
because people are foolish enough
to envy its irony

to. day and night

between love and violence
i sit and have breakfast

to. day and night

i was helplessly brought back to you through
your eyes

in the shadow of a promise
you wait for him all alone
while he takes advantage of the distance
and *heals himself*
the way you would destroy yourself

to. day and night

but instead i sit quietly
i let you choose me
i let you play me
for better reasons
i just do not want you to leave me

to, day and night

NANDINI TIWARI

there are some nights
i sit hidden under the sheets bawling
because of your cruel game of hide and seek

to. day and night

NANDINI TIWARI

as long as my eyes
do not threaten your voice
i will refrain from
gazing into the mirror in search of pleasure

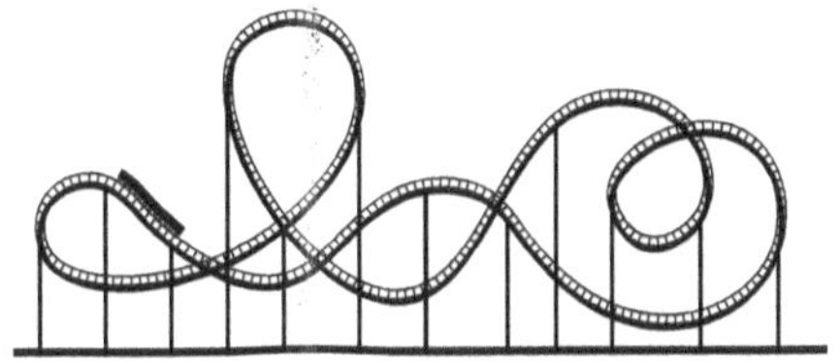

to. day and night

uncover

NANDINI TIWARI

the universe might rob you of joy
it is a constant cycle
call it a friend
and halfway out the door
leave a good man

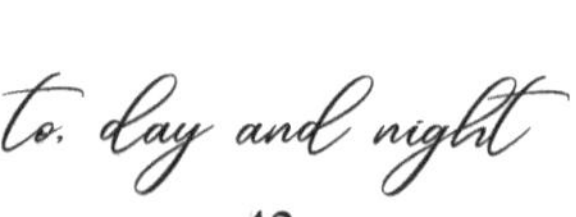

to. day and night

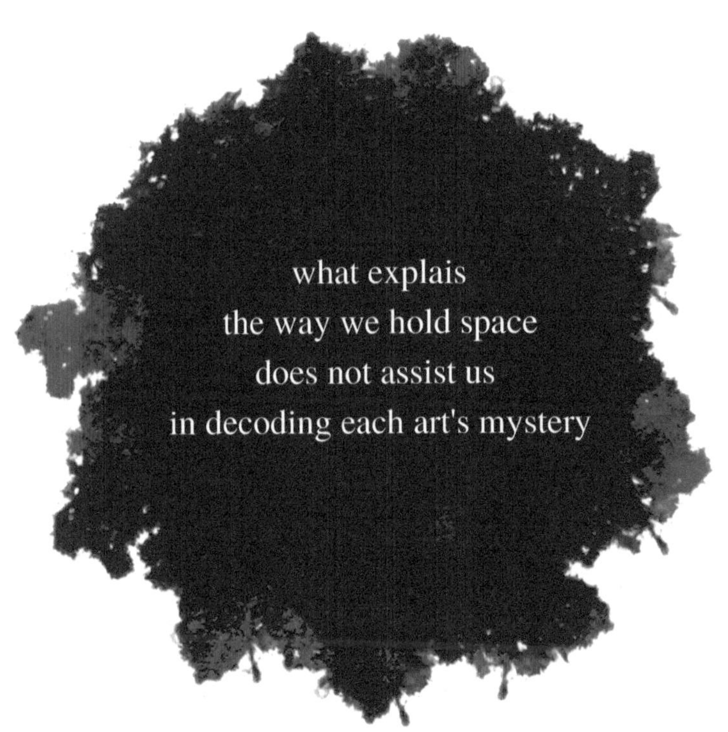
what explais
the way we hold space
does not assist us
in decoding each art's mystery

NANDINI TIWARI

two souls
both a blessing
but parts of her were always hidden

to. day and night

44

NANDINI TIWARI

i'd rather be tired of falling in love
than taste your sweet anger
in this temple
the choice is not yours
my wounds ask for help
and the invisible ones are blinded by fear
the fear of not being perfect

to. day and night

when i reach my end
tell me the secret of us
i want to know why we are all different
so that in my next life
i climb before the heavens withdraw

to. day and night

in the late-night conversations
between magic
when you're down there
i want someone who starves
my internal attention
rather than our connection

to, day and night

NANDINI TIWARI

i would love to understand darkness
with a mirror in between
to make the empty fields
with monsters
understand the two sides of a lie

to. day and night

48

stars are blessed
with the exchange of wounds
and the words that you cannot express

to. day and night

someday someone will teach the moon
all the lies that stand between
him and his universe

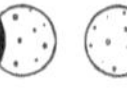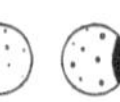

to, day and night

NANDINI TIWARI

it will all be what you want
but i still want to know
if we can do this together
you are focused so i deny
messing up with you
feeling scared to lose you

if i could tell you that i will be different
i would
those eyes hold a special moment for me
it's different than love
in the remaining months i wish
i make this happen
i will take care of you
and be everything in between
i want more
than those five seconds in the morning
and that last minute walk

2am confessions

to. day and night

i am sorry my world split us equal

to. day and night

the spiral of a lover's body
is the smallest hint of love
to chase away tenderness

to, day and night

54

true relationships are characterized
by broken compliments and
love and hate alike

to. day and night

i carry immense energy
within the little space
fulfilling their expectations
to choose what
we deserve

to. day and night

the secrets are busting inside of me
and like the sleepless travellers
i do not care of the time
i will harm the lovers without the warning
and will be afraid of silence

even with that little freedom in these hands
i do not want to resonate my journey
with a hundred voices
burning my thoughts like the trees on fire
i want to suspend pain
and embrace the moon
i want to escape from the painful beauty
of whispers and i want to secretly be jealous
of everything without your supervision
i will not be hidden under the luck
of those beloved answers

i will not be hidden
i will not be hidden

to. day and night

acceptance

NANDINI TIWARI

a walk under the stars
to quickly fill up the conversations
in the jars of hope and courage
for our scars

to, day and night

living in a world
where memories taught me
to be alone on the path of healing
with words that were mistaken as music

to. day and night

NANDINI TIWARI

to complete yourself
is to first believe
that you exist amongst others
with an aura to steal
without gucci flora

to. day and night

it feels like i'm barely living for myself
when it comes to
deciding the cause of beauty

as i communicate through my fingers
i might leave a scar to this young child

to, day and night

NANDINI TIWARI

you deserve happiness
for the love of your childhood mirror
where you felt beautiful in all ways
and never underestimated the joy of colours
i assure you the angels still have your side

what's wrong in giving it a try?
for everyone dies the day he writes

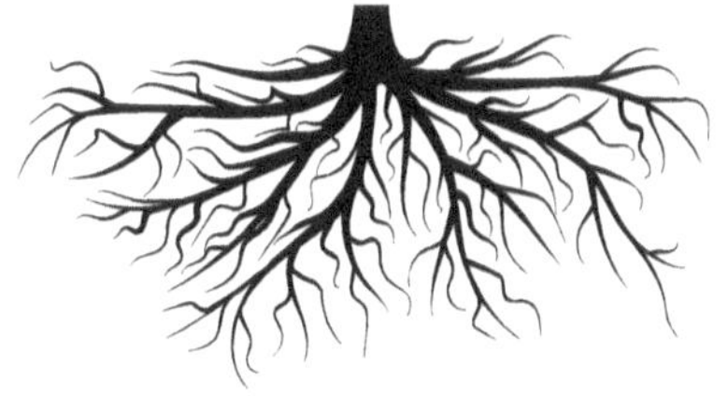

to. day and night

you're perfect on paper like magic
but i wish i could appreciate your characters
unknowingly
forcing myself to deal with it
i want to be loud
i want to be loud to be heard
there are times when i wish
to understand your incomplete stories
of memories
that i want to set on fire
but i am afraid to touch you
i am afraid to touch your heart
because i know it hurts
it hurts to lose and scream
and *it hurts to wake up from a dream*

to. day and night

we might one day be able to make up
in the language of conversations

to, day and night

how silly of me to not be brave enough
to love all my perfect imperfections

to. day and night

we can only work by the laws of nature

when we escape to feel alive

convince yourself into believing
that your future will complete you
into the complement that will heal you

It is the past, the past, my darling!

NANDINI TIWARI

honour your body with those hands
do not let yourself down
know that you're more than capable
of getting tied
and screaming without pleasure
undress yourself
by not worrying about those whispers
of responsibility and
call it love when you
feel safe and speechless

honour your body
for you to heal
love and
spread love

to. day and night

i don't count the minutes to justify a sin
people leave easy to let you break in circles

NANDINI TIWARI

your grief expands with learning
it is an old rule
that provides us with an experience
weeping mercy

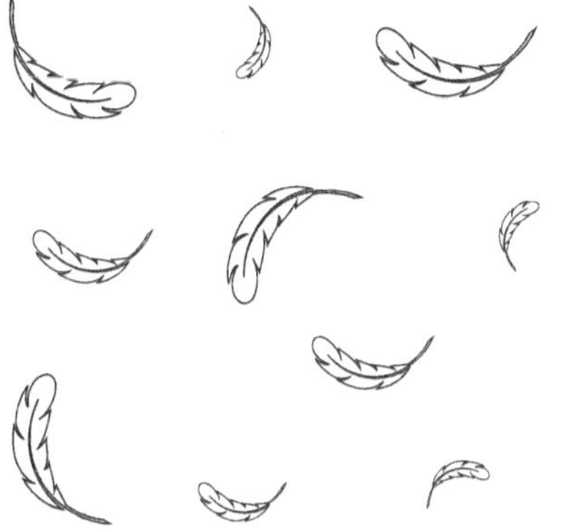

to, day and night

i strive to put myself ahead
of anxiety during breakfast
in order to strike
that exhausted energy

with twenty under my belt
i've given myself space to rest
when my body signals
honour
value and
attention

to. day and night

NANDINI TIWARI

you didn't lose it
in every act of embracing a relationship
what makes it boring
is the unconditional magic of pieces
that fill you up searching for survival

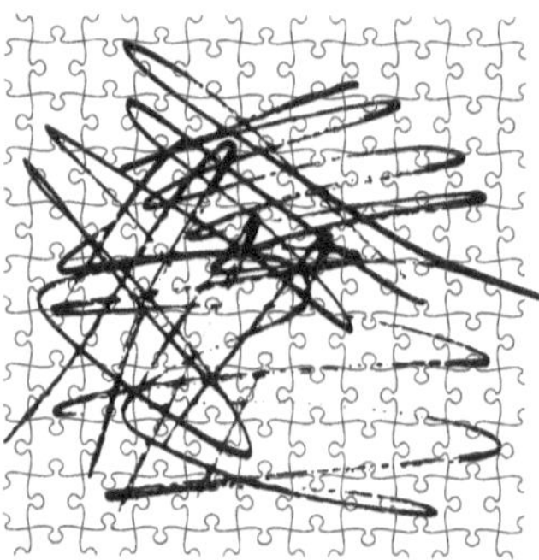

to. day and night

perform

it rewards those
who take advantage
of the system
by pretending to be empty
in order to build a life
full of joy
destroying the returning

to, day and night

NANDINI TIWARI

...her heart burns them
in the stories left incomplete
crowded with the soft thorns of present
her name stands unknown
for us to complete

to. day and night

NANDINI TIWARI

it is scary to connect your soul to mine
and get lost in between that one night
i admire your love for me and my pleasure
wanting to be yours
i let go with maddening hunger
you are important
but some things cannot be built together
i wish i could
let that thought go off my shoulder
our texts will comfort one another
in the memory that will last forever

we started
by being silent
about our choices
in order to be in sync with each other
(in a circle forever)

to. day and night

it is your job to wake up
and renew yourself
in the waves along the streets of aches

i want you to realise
how powerful that one scream can be
to align your mind and body
to help you stay
in the mess with the mirror
under your own breath

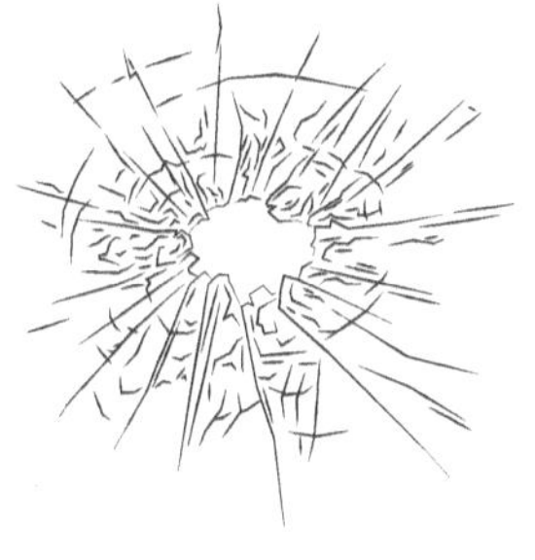

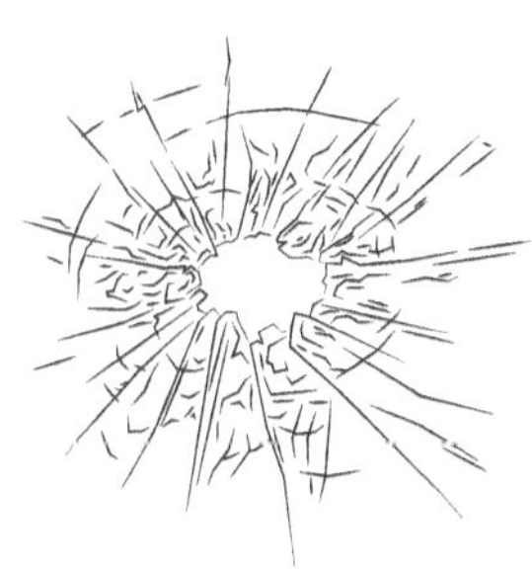

to, day and night

having spent the past week buying products
comparing myself with angels
i roll into the messiness of creativity
to build for them instead

to. day and night

let yourself shine with your love
your words will engrave
in the mystery of the ocean
only when
you are true and pure

to. day and night

it takes death
to climb freedom from all humility

to. day and night

so i wanted to change
against a rule to be so complete
that my name itself
adds fire to his thought

to. day and night

NANDINI TIWARI

she eventually gives up on emptiness
throwing paper planes embraced with chaos

tough enough to reintroduce the universe
with the wishing stars
she quickly pulls herself together

she lives as they grow

regardless of what you need
bloom
dive in deeper between comfort and fear
and let the grace from within
redefine care

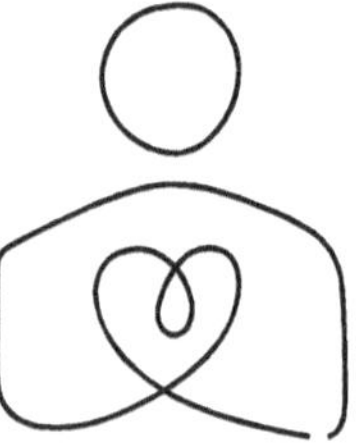

begin with error

to uncover acceptance

while you perform

and after all this
just being called a woman
loudly
lustily
attractively
dangerously and
softly
is a gift

.period.

NANDINI TIWARI

i could light a whole city
but to decorate it
and leave carelessly excites me

for i wonder who the next artist could be?

NANDINI TIWARI

you will one day be free
to rush through
the art gallery of life
without love

you are closer to me than myself
you let it blossom
with the freshness of silence
and the sweetness of blessings
to reason it
you only provide a smile
to be charming and faithful
and block the roads with anger and pride
you let it sink
you let love sink in a secret way
unknown to others
for me to be sure
patient and closer to you
and so i accept you

to. day and night

to, day and night

but most importantly
you were the words of mystery
that lived a lifetime

to, day and night

NANDINI TIWARI

it wasn't for love but for memories
that i wanted to swim until the end
but never did i expect
the star would turn its back on me
and make my journey full of wounds
it caused me to bleed
but with the visible form independence
i was able to form
my own version of reality
i cared and fought for myself
i did fumble upon my flaws
but
i won the wand of stars
i won the wand of stars

to. day and night

NANDINI TIWARI

i hope you find love wrapped around my wrist
under the same sky
on the same night
so that
i wouldn't have to do it all alone
i wouldn't have to love alone

to. day and night

NANDINI TIWARI

i enjoy being alone
burning below the summer sky
to fit in my trapped skin
waving me a goodbye
i will always have
enough energy to heal
but not time
and so i hide behind a constant smile

to. day and night

i prefer to stick to my weaknesses
and wrap myself with desires
to numb the flames of love

to heal within
i apologize to myself and dream of flying
rather being disappointed
at the moment that sit still

this mistake was just
another piece of puzzle
collected to complete
for when the world ends

to. day and night

i can live without the impossible
we can live without the impossible
for the power to fulfil us
lies within the escapism of
daydream and imagination
waiting for the pleasure to be yours
always to be yours

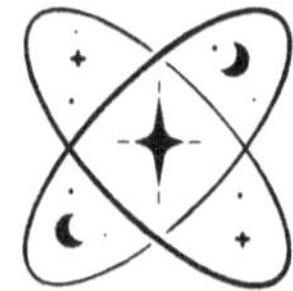

to. day and night

it's now! that you're
worshipping the philosophy
of understanding conversations
between the representation of our story

to. day and night

and somehow every love
turns mysterious
that was once
all about the falling stars family

to. day and night

today this city offers a hundred blessings
that steal the musicians' truth
and plant joy in our livelihood

to. day and night

your pain walks full of grace
onto that holy mountain
knowing the hidden powers
will cure the aura
and let you bloom
to sweeten the branches of dreams
this is where love pays respect before death

to. day and night

NANDINI TIWARI

this isn't a coincidence
written in the language of silence
we share the same heart
and today
i'm not afraid to share my pieces
because this girl now knows what cheating is

to. day and night

while joy accompanies the long night
the greatest honour comes from the
conversation between the guilt of leaving

NANDINI TIWARI

i wrote to them and about them for you

to,
day and night

you're appreciated
the ones who could change me and the ones i
could change for

"i just evolve because life is worth living"

nandini started writing when she was sixteen years old it wasn't easy to endure criticism throughout however giving up was not an option

as she says she feels alive in the world she creates for herself

she believes in compiling every piece of art that consists of words for the world to rest in her sentences and for all to remember her in her independence

*with this book nandini has written her **fifth collection of poetry***

further she is actively involved in the community and runs a non-profit organization

-about the author

join nandini tiwari on

@twarinandini

to, day and night is a
collection of poetry about
the journey of
self-acceptance
love
and growth
it is split into six chapters
begin,error,uncover,acceptance, perform and
begin with error to uncover acceptance while you
perform

the book's final chapter title contains all the words
from the previous chapters which perfectly sums up
the book's theme

-about the book

illustrations- Canva